Study Guide

What Great Teachers Do Differently: 14 Things That Matter Most

Beth Whitaker and Todd Whitaker

EYE ON EDUCATION

6 DEPOT WAY WEST, SUITE 106

LARCHMONT, NY 10538

(914) 833–0551

(914) 833–0761 fax

www.eyeoneducation.com

ISBN 1-59667-024-X

10 9 8 7 6 5 4 3

Editorial and production services provided by
Richard H. Adin Freelance Editorial Services
52 Oakwood Blvd., Poughkeepsie, NY 12603-4112
(845-471-3566)

Table of Contents

Introduction

This *Study Guide* is a tool to accompany *What Great Teachers Do Differently: 14 Things That Matter Most.* It is a practical resource for educators who are examining what great teachers do that sets them apart from others. It focuses on the beliefs, behaviors, attitudes, and commitments that positively impact teaching and learning in our classrooms and our schools.

Note to Facilitators: If you are conducting a book study group, seminar, or professional development event, this *Study Guide* also serves as a roadmap to help you organize and work with your group. It provides assistance to staff developers, principals, team leaders, college professors, and other educational leaders who are working with teachers as they develop their professional skills.

What Great Teachers Do Differently: 14 Things That Matter Most is a slender, but powerful, book. It is not a book comprised of hard scientific data, detailed assessment rubrics, or esoteric theories. Rather, it is a book that clearly, concisely, and accurately informs teachers what it is that our most effective teachers do on a daily basis. Put simply, it is a book that teachers can *use*—and use immediately. The *Study Guide* is written to aid the participants' understanding of the essential concepts described in the book, and to put them to immediate use in their classrooms and schools.

To stress the practicality of the book's contents, each of the twelve sections of the *Study Guide* focuses on one or two chapters of the book and is organized into five parts, with the acronym *USE IT* in mind, as follows:

- *Understanding Key Concepts*, which summarize the key points for each chapter in the book;

- *Selecting Questions for Discussion*, which can be used within the classroom/workshop setting;

- *Eliciting Journal Responses*, which is a prompt for journal writing, based on the specific contents of the chapters;

- *Interacting With Others*, which offers ideas for activities to use with participants; and

- *Taking It Back*, which offers ideas for applying what is learned in the book and class/workshop in the classrooms of our schools.

The authors would like to thank Jeff Zoul for his assistance in the preparation of these materials.

Section One

Chapter 1: Why Look at Great
Chapter 2: It's People,
Not Programs

Understanding Key Concepts

♦ Great teachers do not use sarcasm, yell at students, or argue with students in ff other students.

♦ We can always learn from observing what great teachers do. Eliminating inappropriate choices does not help as much as identifying good ideas used by successful educators.

♦ All that is truly needed to improve education is for *all* teachers to be like our very *best* teachers.

♦ *Who we are* as teachers and *what we do* as teachers is more important than what we know. Teachers must self-reflect on who they are and what they must do in order to improve their practice.

♦ There are really only two ways to improve any school: get better teachers and improve the teachers already there.

♦ No program inherently leads to school improvement. It is the people who implement sound programs and determine the success of the school. Programs are never the solution, and they are never the problem.

♦ What matters most is not *what* teachers do (including "programs" such as whole language, assertive discipline, open classrooms), but *how* appropriately and effectively they do it.

Selecting Questions for Discussion

♦ What is the most important idea communicated in these two chapters? How would you implement this idea in your classroom?

♦ Why should we look at what great teachers do?

♦ Why must we also study less-effective teachers and schools when determining what constitutes great teachers and schools?

♦ What is it that determines—in the eyes of parents and students—whether or not a school is great?

♦ Are *Open Classrooms, Back to Basics, Whole Language,* and *Assertive Discipline* programs inherently good or bad? Explain.

♦ When considering whether or not to adopt a school program change, what should stand as the primary criterion?

♦ Which of the three words in the phrase "poor lecturer's classroom" identifies the problem? How is this single example illustrative of the "people versus programs" concept?

Notes

Eliciting Journal Responses

Think of a program that was implemented in recent years at your school or a school with which you are familiar. Which teachers adapted to the change of programs, embracing the new idea and making it work? Did any teachers resist the change? Was the program ultimately deemed a success? What determined whether or not it was successful?

_____

_____

_____

_____

_____

_____

_____

_____

_____

_____

_____

_____

_____

_____

_____

_____

_____

_____

_____

_____

_____

_____

Interacting With Others

Teaching 5th grade for 38 years

In groups of three to five, consider the following two points: (a) Some teachers have 20 years of teaching experience; others who have taught for 20 years have 1 year of experience which they have repeated 20 times. (b) "Students want to know how much you care before they care how much you know." On p. 7 of the book, there is a description of a teacher who taught the same grade effectively for 38 years. Use the scenarios above and discuss how they apply to this particular teacher. Create a list with three categories: *what she knew* as a teacher, *who she was* as a teacher, and *what she did* as a teacher. Based on the description of this effective veteran teacher, brainstorm descriptions within each category that would likely have applied to her and her knowledge, passion, and practices as an educator. Be prepared to share these lists with the group.

It's not what you do, it's how you do it

Beginning on p. 10 of the book, three "programs" are described that are deemed neither a problem nor a solution: Open Classrooms, Assertive Discipline, and Lecturing. Divide participants into three groups and assign each group one section ("How Open Classrooms Got Started," "Assertive Discipline—The Problem or the Solution," and "The Poor Lecturer's Classroom") to review. Have each group create and present a skit to the entire group showing how the "program" in question can be both an effective and ineffective strategy in teaching.

Notes

Taking It Back

In his book *Good To Great: Why Some Companies Make the Leap…and Others Don't*, Jim Collins maintains that good is actually the enemy of great; that is, we have so few *great* companies because so many are willing to settle for being *good* companies. He extends the examples to schools, indicating that we have so few great schools primarily because we have good schools. The book, too, speaks to the shade of difference between good and great teachers, stating that most teachers do about as well as they know how. Maintaining anonymity, identify two teachers who are settling for good and two teachers who always strive for greatness. What is the obvious difference between the two pairs? Write your insights and reflect on what the great teachers are doing differently than those classified as merely "good." Share these observations at the next session.

_____

_____

_____

_____

_____

_____

_____

_____

_____

_____

_____

_____

_____

_____

_____

_____

_____

_____

_____

_____

Section Two

Chapter 3: The Power of Expectations

Understanding Key Concepts

- Great teachers focus on expectations, other teachers focus on rules, and the least-effective teachers focus on the consequences of breaking the rules.
- Great teachers establish clear expectations at the outset of the school year and follow them firmly, fairly, and consistently throughout the year.
- Rules have drawbacks, including their focus on undesirable behaviors, whereas expectations focus on desirable behaviors.
- Teachers may have varying expectations, but all great teachers set expectations which are clearly established, focused on the future, and consistently reinforced.

Selecting Questions for Discussion

♦ What is the most important idea communicated in this chapter regarding teacher expectations?

♦ What are the advantages and disadvantages of spelling out specific consequences for breaking rules?

♦ What is, at times, a more powerful deterrent to misbehavior than a list of predetermined rules and consequences?

♦ Why is it vitally important that teachers establish clear expectations at the beginning of the school year?

♦ In addition to setting clear expectations for students each year, why do great teachers set expectations each new school year for themselves, too?

Eliciting Journal Responses

Take a moment to consider what is vitally important to you as a teacher in terms of managing your classroom and setting expectations so that students in your classroom learn and behave to the best of their ability and to your level of expectation. Decide on no more than three to five items and state these as expectations for students. Brainstorm in writing how you can communicate these expectations clearly, ensure that these expectations are consistently reinforced, and how you will react when students fail to meet them.

_____

_____

_____

_____

_____

_____

_____

_____

_____

_____

_____

_____

_____

_____

_____

_____

_____

_____

_____

_____

_____

_____

_____

_____

Interacting With Others

Stop the thumping!

On p. 18 of the book, a scenario is described whereby the school principal only adds to the "problem" of thumping by announcing an edict regarding such behavior during the middle of an instructional period. In groups of five to seven, come up with another way in which teachers actually create additional misbehavior by focusing on currently occurring misbehaviors. Each group should act out this classroom scenario for the group at large. After each group presents, discuss ways in which the misbehavior could have been handled differently.

Expectations, rules, consequences

Post three large pieces of chart paper around the room labeled "Expectations," "Rules," and "Consequences." In pairs, have participants brainstorm as many examples as possible for each category. Ask one member of the group to record with a marker each response on all three charts, listing each item only once, but placing a sticker next to items each time it is repeated. Allow time for each pair to share their lists to be included on the charts. After all responses have been recorded, take time to note which list is the largest and smallest. Does this tell us anything? Are there any "rules" listed that we can live without or that can be restated as an expectation? Are there any "consequences" listed that seem unnecessary? Are there other, less-punitive options that have not been included as a consequence? Are all items listed as "expectations" truly expectations or did some "rules" sneak onto this list? Remember that the order of emphasis when ranking these three items should be expectations, rules, consequences.

Notes

Taking It Back

Visit three to five classrooms at different grade levels throughout your school. Take note of any classroom rules, guidelines, expectations, and consequences that are posted in the room. Take special notice of the positive and productive examples you observe. Analyze what you find in light of the information presented in Chapter 3. Compare this analysis with your own classroom. Can you make any adjustments to your own practice based upon your observations? Be prepared to share your findings at the next session.

_____

_____

_____

_____

_____

_____

_____

_____

_____

_____

_____

_____

_____

_____

_____

_____

_____

_____

_____

_____

_____

Section Three

Chapter 4:
Prevention Versus Revenge

Understanding Key Concepts

- Effective teachers are motivated to prevent misbehavior; ineffective teachers are motivated to punish students who misbehave.
- Effective teachers focus on the future and what they have the ability to influence, not on what has already happened.
- Angry students are a problem, not a solution. When a student misbehaves, effective teachers do not want a student to leave the classroom angry, they want the student to behave better in the future.
- All teachers have the same "bag of tricks" available to them in dealing with student behavior.
- The variable is the teacher—great teachers choose wisely from this bag of tricks.
- Students know the difference between right and wrong and want the teacher to address inappropriate behavior in a dignified and respectful manner.

Selecting Questions for Discussion

- Discuss the differences in how effective and ineffective teachers react when a student misbehaves.

- What do effective teachers need from the principal when they send a student to the office? Explain the significance of this need.

- What are some variables that separate effective classroom managers from ineffective classroom managers?

- What must teachers do to keep students on their side in supporting appropriate classroom behavior?

- Identify at least five specific teacher behaviors in every teacher's bag of tricks that great teachers never exhibit.

Eliciting Journal Responses

Reflect back on a situation (or imagine a situation) in your classroom when, despite your best efforts to clearly establish proactive expectations, a student still misbehaved to the point that you were compelled to refer the student to a school administrator. Write about what behavior prompted the office referral and the result of the student's visit to the office. Did the student's behavior change? Did the student come back from the office angry? How did you follow up on the misbehavior upon the student's return to the classroom in the days that followed? In hindsight, would you have changed how you handled the misbehavior?

_____

_____

_____

_____

_____

_____

_____

_____

_____

_____

_____

_____

_____

_____

_____

_____

_____

_____

Interacting With Others

A bag of tricks

On page 25, the book explains that all teachers have similar options in dealing with student misbehavior, but that great teachers differ from ineffective teachers both in the quantity and quality of "tricks" they employ. Distribute ten slips of paper to each member of the study group. Each participant should list ten different options available to teachers when dealing with student misbehavior, one on each slip of paper. These should be placed in a bag in the front of the room. After all slips have been completed and placed in the bag, take a moment and "pull several tricks from the bag." After each pull, take a minute to discuss the relative merits of the option, and how many people placed the same or similar option in the bag. End with a discussion of when and how often the study group would choose an office referral as the appropriate action.

The top 20

Read the list of 20 statements related to classroom management below. In small groups, rank the list in order of importance for establishing an orderly and respectful learning environment. Ask volunteers to share their top five and explain why they chose these items.

- I am friendly but firm with my students.
- I treat each student with kindness and respect.
- When a student or students act inappropriately, I remain calm and composed.
- I display enthusiasm and a sense of humor with my students.
- I give my students a pleasing greeting each day and wish them a pleasant weekend.
- So that I know what is going on in my classroom, I generally spend my class time on my feet.
- When I correct student misbehavior, I communicate in a private, positive, and respectful manner.
- I admit that at times student misbehavior is a result of something that was my fault.
- I carefully plan each lesson so that there is no "dead time."
- I adjust my daily lesson planning to take into account my students' span of attention.

- I think through discipline decisions before acting.

- I make only those discipline decisions that I can enforce.

- I make discipline decisions after the "heat of the moment" has passed.

- When a student misbehaves in class, I find a way to correct the behavior privately, perhaps by moving near the student and whispering a correction.

- While I take attendance or perform other necessary tasks, often at the outset of each class session, my students are working independently, perhaps on a brief assignment or problem on the overhead or board.

- I establish time-saving routines for collecting papers and distributing materials or supplies.

- I show sincere enthusiasm for the subjects I teach.

- I provide a neat classroom that gives students the idea of orderliness.

- I present a professional appearance in the classroom.

- I insist that my students maintain high standards in their work and behavior. In both areas, my standards are realistic and attainable.

Notes

Taking It Back

Please complete the following survey individually as a way to self-reflect on your individual discipline practices. Respond with a 1 to 4 ranking, with 4 indicating "Almost Always," 3 indicating "Frequently," 2 indicating "Occasionally," and 1 indicating "Almost Never." You will be asked to share what you learned about yourself as a professional educator as a result of completing this at the next session.

1. I am friendly but firm with my students. _____

2. I treat each student with kindness and respect. _____

3. When a student or students act inappropriately, I remain calm and composed. _____

4. I display enthusiasm and a sense of humor with my students. _____

5. During each passing period between classes, I am at the doorway to greet and chat with students. _____

6. I interact with all students, not just a few. _____

7. I give my students a pleasing greeting each day and wish them a pleasant weekend. _____

8. During each passing period between classes, I am at the doorway so I can supervise both the hallway and my classroom. _____

9. So that I know what is going on in my classroom, I generally spend my class time on my feet. _____

10. I expect students to listen attentively when another student or I am talking. _____

11. When I correct student misbehavior, I communicate in a private, positive, and respectful manner. _____

12. I admit that at times student misbehavior is a result of something that was my fault. _____

13. I am able to motivate my students, including the reluctant learner. _____

14. I carefully plan each lesson so that there is no "dead time." _____

15. I provide guided or independent practice during which I move about the room offering individual or small group assistance. _____

16. During each class period, I provide a variety of learning activities. Rarely do I use an entire period for a single activity, as students need a change of pace. _____

17. I adjust my daily lesson planning to take into account my students' span of attention. _____

18. I think through discipline decisions before acting.   _____

19. I make only those discipline decisions that I can enforce.   _____

20. I make discipline decisions after the "heat of the moment" has
    passed.   _____

21. When a student misbehaves in class, I find a way to correct the
    behavior privately, perhaps by moving near the student and
    whispering a correction.   _____

22. While I take attendance or perform other necessary tasks, often
    at the outset of each class session, my students are working
    independently, perhaps on a brief assignment or problem on the
    overhead or board.   _____

23. I establish time saving routines for collecting papers and distrib-
    uting materials or supplies.   _____

24. My directions for a learning activity are brief and concise.   _____

25. I give directions one step at a time. I avoid long and detailed
    directions.   _____

26. I show sincere enthusiasm for the subjects I teach.   _____

27. I provide a neat classroom that gives students the idea of
    orderliness.   _____

28. I present a professional appearance in the classroom.   _____

29. I insist that my students maintain high standards in their work
    and behavior. In both areas, my standards are realistic and
    attainable.   _____

30. Because there is no "best" teaching method, my methods and
    learning activities are many and varied.   _____

31. My homework assignments have a purpose, are instructional,
    and are regulated as to the time it will take a student to complete
    the assignment.   _____

32. I make my classroom attractive by having effective bulletin
    boards related to the topics being studied at the particular time.   _____

33. During each class session, I summarize, or have students sum-
    marize, the day's learning.   _____

34. I use pretests or other procedures to ascertain what students
    already know.   _____

Section Four

Chapter 5: High Expectations—For Whom?
Chapter 6: Who Is the Variable?

Understanding Key Concepts

- All teachers have high expectations for students, even ineffective teachers. The difference is that great teachers also have very high expectations of themselves.
- It is easy to have high expectations for others; the challenge for teachers is to focus on their own behavior.
- When students are not focused and engaged in the classroom, great teachers ask themselves what *they* can do differently to improve student engagement.
- The main variable in any classroom is not the students, but the teacher.
- Effective teachers always strive to improve and they focus on something they can control: their own behavior.
- Just as successful students and parents accept responsibility, our most effective teachers accept responsibility for their performance in the classroom.

Selecting Questions for Discussion

♦ What is the variable in terms of teacher expectations?

♦ Do you believe that most principals and fellow teachers can predict which teachers will send the most students to the office each year? Explain.

♦ How do ineffective teachers and effective teachers react when their students do poorly on an assessment? Is there a difference? If so, why?

♦ Why do successful teachers insist on focusing on their own behavior rather than the behavior of others (e.g., parents, administrators, students)?

♦ How are effective teachers similar to the effective business managers the book mentions?

Eliciting Journal Responses

Throughout these two chapters, the book stresses the belief that teachers should take responsibility for what happens within their classrooms. It suggests that if we all look in the mirror each time we ask "Who is the variable?," we will have taken great strides toward school improvement. Take a few moments to write about your thoughts on this concept. Next, take some time to reflect in writing about how the issues of student, parent, and teacher responsibility all play a significant role in ensuring academic success for each student we teach.

_____

_____

_____

_____

_____

_____

_____

_____

_____

_____

_____

_____

_____

_____

_____

_____

_____

_____

_____

_____

_____

Interacting With Others

Expectations—for everyone

In an earlier journal entry, you were asked to list three to five expectations for student behavior that you deemed of vital importance. Working in groups of two to five, reexamine the issue of expectations from the perspective of students and parents. Identify several expectations for which all stakeholders should hold all teachers accountable. List these as "We will…" statements, as in: "*We* (as teachers) *will* treat all members of our school community with dignity and respect." Write five "We will…" statements to which you, as a stakeholder, would expect teachers to adhere. You will be asked to share your list, recording answers on the board, overhead, chart paper, or computer screen. After each group has shared, you will need to decide which of these "We will…" statements you believe to be the five most important.

Mission, vision, values

You will have the opportunity to view numerous mission, vision, and value statements from various sources. These examples come from schools, businesses, and other organizations. Discuss, as a group, the definition and differences among the three commonly used terms: *Mission*—what is our purpose; *Vision*—what do we hope to become; and *Values*—what commitments are we willing to adopt in order to make our vision a reality. You need to divide into three groups: a "Mission" group, a "Vision" group, and a "Values" group. The groups will work together to create a mission, vision, and value statement for a great teacher. After sharing these group statements, you will create your own individual mission, vision, and value statements for yourself as a classroom teacher.

Notes

Taking It Back

On return to your classrooms, engage in instructional self-reflection for a full week. At the end of each day, identify the one teaching/instructing activity that did not go as well as you had envisioned. After the lesson is identified, list three adjustments you will make so that the next time you teach that lesson it will be successful for the learners. Looking at oneself is always the first reflective step of a great teacher. In the next session, you will have the opportunity to discuss your progress made while completing this weeklong instructional reflection activity.

Section Five

Chapter 7:
Ten Days Out of Ten

Understanding Key Concepts

- Great teachers create a positive atmosphere each day in their classrooms despite inevitable negatives such as irate parents, troubled students, and limited resources.
- Effective teachers treat everyone with dignity and respect ten days out of ten. They may not like all their students, but they *act* as if they do.
- Students may remember the times teachers treat them well, but they will *always* remember when they were treated disrespectfully or unfairly—even if it is only one time.
- Effective teachers understand the power of praise and look for opportunities to find people doing things right.
- To be effective, praise must be *authentic, specific, immediate, clean,* and *private.*
- Focusing on all the positive things in our classrooms and schools gives us more drive and energy to get through the less-positive times.
- Effective teachers know that one of the most important tasks that a teacher performs is to model appropriate behavior. Consequently, great teachers model the behavior of treating all people with dignity and respect all the time.

Selecting Questions for Discussion

♦ Why must great teachers always act as if they like all of their students?

♦ Define the five necessary components of effective praise: authentic, specific, immediate, clean, and private. Explain why each is important and provide an example.

♦ Which of the five components of effective praise is often the most challenging for educators? Why?

♦ Who determines how much you praise someone? Who feels better each time you do?

♦ Identify three myths that are often used as rationalizations of why we do not praise more often. Offer an argument that debunks each myth.

Notes

Eliciting Journal Responses

Each of us can recall an occasion in our professional life when someone in a leadership role treated us inappropriately. Think of such a time in your own adult life when this happened. Is it etched into your memory? Can you recall a similar situation from your own school career in grades K–12 when a teacher made a cutting remark or acted rudely toward you? Describe a situation from that time and how it made you feel. Did it change your opinion of that particular teacher?

_____

_____

_____

_____

_____

_____

_____

_____

_____

_____

_____

_____

_____

_____

_____

_____

_____

_____

_____

_____

_____

_____

_____

Interacting With Others

The power of praise

On pp. 46–49, the book details Bissell's five traits that help praise work, noting that, to be effective, praise must be *authentic, specific, immediate, clean, and private.* After organizing the into several groups, ask one group to portray a classroom scene in which a teacher praises "students" while clearly demonstrating authenticity, specificity, immediacy, cleanliness, and privacy. Have other groups portray an example of a teacher using praise, but breaking one of the five requirements of effective praise. Ask the nonperforming participants to identify which of the five requirements was violated. After all of these portrayals have been presented, discuss what you think is the most important of the five characteristics of effective praise.

Our cup runneth over!

In this chapter, the book emphasizes that focusing on the positive elements of our classrooms and schools will give us more drive and energy as we face our daily work. Divide into groups of three to five. Each group will be provided with a piece of chart paper with a large cup or glass drawn on it and a package of sticky notes. You are to "fill" your cup with examples of great things happening in your classrooms and schools. Write brief thoughts and descriptions on the sticky notes and place them inside the cup. Continue working until each cup is filled with the positive, productive things happening in your schools. Allow time for individuals to share inside the groups. Then each group must choose and share its "Top 5" positive ideas with the entire group. Post these charts for all to read and discuss.

Notes

Taking It Back

On page 51, the book notes that one reason teachers give for not praising more is lack of time. Make the time during the next five school days to praise at least five different students and five different colleagues. For the students, this should be in the form of a phone call to parents praising a specific behavior or accomplishment, or a postcard or handwritten note sent home in the mail. For colleagues, this might be done in the form of a positive note placed in teacher mailboxes. You will be asked to report back at the next session your reaction to this activity, as well as, the reactions of the people you praised.

_____

_____

_____

_____

_____

_____

_____

_____

_____

_____

_____

_____

_____

_____

_____

_____

_____

_____

_____

Section Six

Chapter 8:
The Teacher Is the Filter

Understanding Key Concepts

- The teacher is the filter who sets the tone for how others behave. If the tone teachers establish is positive and professional, students will match that tone; if our attitude is negative and confrontational, students will respond in kind.

- The principal's goal for faculty meetings should be to make teachers more excited about teaching tomorrow than they are today. Great teachers take the same approach for their class: Great teachers want students to be more excited about learning tomorrow than they are today.

- Great teachers realize that teaching is a demanding job, yet they focus on its rewards and challenges in a positive way instead of complaining.

- The best teachers are professionals who know to keep personal issues private and also know to keep school issues in their place. They do not involve students in inappropriate topics.

- Our own perception of our school and our students impacts the reality of our school and students. Teachers have the power to decide the tone of their school and how teachers in their school view their students.

Selecting Questions for Discussion

♦ In what ways do teachers serve as "filters" in the schools in which they teach?

♦ How can not sharing information with colleagues create a more productive environment?

♦ Explain the statement, "When the teacher sneezes, the whole class catches a cold."

♦ How can great teachers counteract colleagues who are prone to complaining about school, teaching, students, and administration?

♦ Examine the often heard refrain, "This is the worst group of kids we've ever had." Why do some teachers say this? What are the effects of saying this? How can we change this mentality? How does it make you feel when you jear or say it?

Eliciting Journal Responses

Take a moment to consider the negative comments you might hear during the course of a school week from students, other teachers, administrators, and parents. Recall from the book that by constantly filtering out such negatives that do not matter and by, instead, sharing a positive attitude, we can create a more successful school environment. Write about typical negatives you might hear from any of these groups of school stakeholders and how, in the future, you could filter out such comments and even alter these perceptions by offering a different perception.

_____

_____

_____

_____

_____

_____

_____

_____

_____

_____

_____

_____

_____

_____

_____

_____

_____

_____

_____

Interacting With Others

Circle of friends

Arrange your study group into two circles—an "inner" circle and an "outer" circle—one inside the other, with the participants in the inner circle facing the people in the outer circle. Have each person in the inner circle relate an example of negativity at his or her school. Have the person in the outer circle who is facing the speaking participant listen carefully and offer suggestions for dealing with this difficult and negative person and/or situation. After approximately five minutes, have the inner circle rotate three places to the right. Repeat the activity, but this time reverse the roles and have the person in the outer circle share a negative scenario and the inner-circle person offer suggestions. Repeat one or two additional times. Then, as a large group, share what was learned. Did most participants share similar stories? What were the most useful strategies for dealing with negative people/situations?

Filtering out the insignificant

Read this sentence:

> FINISHED FILES ARE THE RESULTS OF YEARS OF SCIENTIFIC STUDY COMBINED WITH THE EXPERIENCE OF YEARS.

Now, count aloud the Fs in the sentence and count them only once. Do not look back and count them again.

How many did you count? Many people count three or four, but there are actually six. The reason that nearly everyone undercounts is because the mind automatically *filters out* the F's in the word *of*, which is included three times in the sentence. Pair up with another participant and discuss how this activity is analogous to filtering out the negatives at school. Like the word *of*, negativity is rampant; if we focused on every *of* or every negative thing we hear, we would miss the big picture—the meaning of what it is we are involved in, whether that is reading or teaching.

Notes

Taking It Back

On your return to your work environment, make a conscious decision to filter out the negative situations that you face, whether they come from within or outside the school. Respond cheerfully to any colleague who asks you how you are doing. Politely dismiss any negative comments made by your teaching peers. Brag about your students each day to anyone who will listen. Tell your students at the end of each day that you can't wait to return to school the following day because you are so excited about what they will be learning tomorrow. After doing this for several consecutive days, *record in your Study Guide* any changes you noticed in your own perspective or that of others, including your students and colleagues.

_____

_____

_____

_____

_____

_____

_____

_____

_____

_____

_____

_____

_____

_____

_____

_____

_____

_____

_____

Section Seven

Chapter 9:
Don't Need to Repair–
Always Do

Understanding Key Concepts

♦ Effective educators know that a relationship, once damaged, may never be the same.

♦ The best teachers seldom need to do any emotional repairing in their classrooms, but they are continually working to repair, just in case.

♦ Great teachers learn to say "I am so sorry that happened" as a way to defuse tense situations and repair relationships.

♦ Great teachers practice behaviors for repairing a situation; they also teach students behaviors for repairing, rather than escalating, a negative situation.

♦ Great teachers work hard to keep their relationships healthy—to avoid personal hurt and to repair any possible damage—and other people notice this.

Selecting Questions for Discussion

◆ What is likely to happen in the classroom when educators become impatient and unprofessional?

◆ Discuss several ways that an effective teacher consistently works to repair relationships.

◆ Why might an effective teacher apologize to a class the day after a less-than-ideal lesson?

◆ Why do less-effective teachers not recognize the need to repair and why do they seldom work to repair? How can we work to change this pattern of behavior in ourselves and/or in others?

◆ Why is the simple act of saying "I am sorry that happened" such a powerful tool?

◆ Why do effective teachers take advantage of teachable moments to help students build the skill of repairing?

Eliciting Journal Responses

Imagine (or draw on your own experience) a situation in which a parent is visibly upset with you about something that happened at school involving the parent's son or daughter (e.g., a bad grade, a demeaning comment which was allegedly made about the child, a punishment with which they did not agree). Write about this situation and how it would play out if your immediate response had been "I am sorry that happened." Write out a script of responses and followup replies in such a situation. Remember that you are not saying it was your fault or accepting blame; rather, you are simply starting off by expressing your sorrow that it happened.

_____

_____

_____

_____

_____

_____

_____

_____

_____

_____

_____

_____

_____

_____

_____

_____

_____

_____

_____

_____

_____

_____

_____

Interacting With Others

The builder

Read the poem "The Builder," which is reprinted below. In pairs, discuss how the themes of the poem relate to the themes of chapter 9 (i.e., "repairing" and "building"). Try your hand at rewriting the poem for the role of a teacher, creating ten rhyming couplets, but keeping the final couplet as it is in its current form. Remember that as teachers we have tremendous influence to build up or tear down our students. We must commit to the role of serving as a builder and repairer, rather than one who tears down. Share your newly created poems with the whole group.

The Builder

I saw a group of men tearing a building down,
A group of men in my hometown.
With a heave and a ho and a mighty yell,
They swung a beam and a side wall fell.
And I said to the foreman, "Are those men skilled?
The type you'd hire if you wanted to build?"
He laughed and replied, "Why, no indeed."
He said, "Common labor is all I need.
Why I can tear down in a day or two
What it takes a builder ten years to do."
And I thought to myself as I walked away,
Which of these roles am I going to play?

(*Author Unknown*)

A restorative approach

The book advises educators to teach students to behave in a way that "restores" them in the eyes of the offended party. In a traditional approach to discipline, the focus may be on (a) what happened, (b) who's to blame, and (c) what's the punishment? On the other hand, a restorative approach asks: (a) What happened? (b) Who has been affected and how? (c) How can we put it right? and (d) What have we learned so that we can make different choices next time? Organize into four groups and give each group a card that has a school setting scenario that might occur where someone is adversely affected. Situations might include a student consistently talks out in class; a student responds disrespectfully to a teacher; a student refuses to complete an assignment; and a student uses inappropriate or threatening language toward a classmate. Have each group analyze its assigned scenario and plan out two courses of action, one based on the traditional approach and one on the restorative approach. Post each group's two plans on two different pieces of chart paper and discuss the benefits and disadvantages of each approach while focusing on the goals of restoration and repairing with the whole group.

Notes

Taking It Back

On page 70 of the book, the author describes an incident involving the highway patrol, in which he describes his goal after having been stopped for speeding—to get out of the ticket. Ask your students if they have ever been in a situation in which they were about to get in big trouble, but managed to minimize the consequence. Relate the story the author tells, tweaking it as appropriate to fit the situation at hand. Teach the students behavior strategies for getting out of trouble—or at least minimizing the severity of the consequence—as you share this story. Emphasize to the students the importance of apologizing and treating the offended party with dignity and respect. Observe the students' reactions and note whether or not any student employs these behaviors in ensuing days. This activity will be discussed in the next session.

_____

_____

_____

_____

_____

_____

_____

_____

_____

_____

_____

_____

_____

_____

_____

_____

_____

_____

_____

_____

Section Eight

Chapter 10:
Ability to Ignore

Understanding Key Concepts

- Great teachers are aware of almost everything that happens in their classroom, and they know which situations demand immediate attention and which can wait for a more appropriate moment.
- Effective teachers model self-control; their classroom management is grounded in their ability to manage their own behavior.
- Great teachers do not automatically react every time a student steps a little out of line.
- The great teacher has the ability to pay attention to students, to recognize and praise their achievements, and the ability to overlook minor errors.
- High achievers put so much of themselves into what they do that any criticism, no matter how minor, can become a personal affront. This is true of high-achieving students and of high-achieving teachers.

Selecting Questions for Discussion

♦ Why do great teachers ignore certain behaviors?

♦ Why do most students misbehave?

♦ What is the likely outcome when we, as educators, continually nit-pick at a child's behavior? At a child's academic performance?

♦ In what ways does the information in this chapter relate specifically to high achievers?

♦ How do great teachers balance the contradictory themes of ignoring certain behaviors and paying attention to those students who crave it?

Notes

Eliciting Journal Responses

The author shares with us the advice of a friend who is a police officer: "You can look for trouble or you can look away." Similarly, William James famously theorized that "[t]he art of being wise is knowing what to overlook." Take a moment to write your reactions to these two quotes as they relate to the classroom setting. What are behaviors that we should regularly overlook which often occur in the classroom? When should we go with the flow and when should we stop and take a stand? How do you determine which disturbances are trivial and should be ignored and which should be responded to? When responding, how do you do so without escalating the situation?

Interacting With Others

When to ignore; when to intervene

Working in groups of three to four, review the following two lists suggesting when to ignore certain behaviors and when to intervene. After reading and discussing both lists thoroughly, read the list of 10 behaviors that follows and determine which of these behaviors you would ignore and which you believe require intervention. Each group will report back to the large group. Group responses will be compared and contrasted.

- ◆ Pointers for When to Ignore Behavior
  - When the inappropriate behavior is unintentional or unlikely to recur.
  - When the goal of a misbehavior is to gain attention.
  - When you want a behavior to decrease.
  - When there is nothing you can do.
- ◆ Pointers for When to Intervene:
  - When there is physical danger or harm to yourself, others, or the child.
  - When a student disrupts the classroom.
  - When there is interference with learning.
  - When the inappropriate behavior will spread to other students.

Ignore	Intervene	Behavior
		Billy Bob is repeatedly tapping his pencil on his desk and is disturbing other students in the classroom.
		Each day Sallie Mae enters the classroom she always kicks the trash can, causing the rest of the class to laugh.
		A student enters the classroom and unintentionally kicks the trash can.
		Jim gets out of his seat to sharpen his pencil.
		Joanna blurts out the response to a question without raising her hand.
		A student is yanking on the ponytail of a student seated in front of him.

		A student calls another student a "fatso" while lining up for lunch.
		During her independent reading time, a student is silently reading the assignment but has a Power Ranger displayed on her desk.
		A student is writing on the surface of her desk with a permanent marker.

To ignore or not to ignore

In groups of five to seven, have each group prepare a skit representing a classroom situation. Each group's scene should include three student misbehaviors, two of which the group believes an effective teacher would ignore and one that the group believes an effective teacher would deal with. In each presentation, the assigned teacher is to "deal" with all three behaviors. After the "lesson," have the other groups predict which of the three behaviors was the one that merited a teacher response.

Notes

Taking It Back

Arrange for someone at your school to videotape you teaching for approximately 15 to 30 minutes. After this is complete, review the tape and conduct a self-analysis of your teaching behaviors, paying particular attention to the way in which you responded—or chose not to respond—to student misbehavior. Make a written record of the strengths and weaknesses you observed in terms of maintaining positive classroom management. Make a second videotape several weeks later and compare your analysis of it with your analysis of the earlier tape.

_____

_____

_____

_____

_____

_____

_____

_____

_____

_____

_____

_____

_____

_____

_____

_____

_____

_____

_____

_____

Section Nine

Chapter 11:
Random or Plandom?
Chapter 12: Base Every Decision on the Best People

- Great teachers have a plan and purpose for everything they do. They reflect on what did and did not work and adjust accordingly.
- Great teachers take responsibility for what happens and plan for success. Less-effective teachers allow classroom events to happen randomly and then blame others when things do not work out well.
- Great teachers expect and plan for appropriate student behavior by ensuring that certain students do—or do not—work together. Great teachers proactively anticipate student misbehavior and plan to eliminate it before it occurs.
- Great teachers intentionally arrange, rearrange, alter, and adjust the structures that frame their teaching. Their classroom setup, their instructional approaches, and their time management are all carefully planned to promote an optimal learning environment.
- Great teachers do not try to prove who is in charge of their classrooms; everyone already knows.
- Great teachers make decisions based on three simple guidelines: (a) What is the purpose? (b) Will this actually accomplish the purpose? (c) What will the best people think?
- Great teachers always treat students as if the students' parents were in the room. They deal with students who disrupt learning, but do so respectfully.
- Great teachers do not "teach to the middle." Instead, they ensure that every student is engaged. They ask, "What will my best students think?" and teach all students accordingly, with the best, most well-rounded students at the forefront when making decisions.

Selecting Questions for Discussion

♦ What is the most important idea communicated in these two chapters? How would you implement this idea in your classroom?

♦ How do great teachers respond when classroom events do not occur as planned?

♦ How do great teachers differ from ineffective teachers in terms of preventing and dealing with student misbehavior?

♦ Name the three simple guidelines great teachers use when making decisions.

♦ Why is it important to focus on the purpose, and not the reason, when making decisions?

♦ Why should teachers avoid "teaching to the middle" of the class?

♦ How do great teachers change the dynamics of a classroom without engaging in power struggles?

♦ What do the best students expect teachers to do about student misbehavior?

Notes

Eliciting Journal Responses

Think of a teacher you know—or who taught you—in whose classroom events always seemed carefully planned. Was this teacher effective? Describe a teacher you had or know who always considers his or her very best students when making decisions regarding teaching and learning. How do you feel your teaching approach would compare to this teacher's?

_____

_____

_____

_____

_____

_____

_____

_____

_____

_____

_____

_____

_____

_____

_____

_____

_____

_____

_____

_____

_____

_____

Interacting With Others

Graffiti on the walls

On page 92 of the book, there is a reference to a school whose principal ordered the bathroom stall doors removed to prevent students from writing on the stalls. In small groups, discuss what the purpose was for this decision. Will this decision accomplish the goal? Next, discuss in small groups how the best students will feel as a result of this decision. Finally, brainstorm in small groups other ways to eradicate the problem of graffiti on the bathroom walls, keeping in mind whether or not the proposed action will accomplish the purpose and what the best students will think of your plan. Have each group share their ideas with the whole group.

More math homework

Imagine that you are teaching at a school in which recent standardized assessments suggest that students are performing well-below average in math. As a result, the principal has directed all teachers to assign more math homework daily. Accepting the assumption that all teachers must comply with this directive, think about the best way to move forward, keeping in mind the purpose, whether or not it will accomplish the purpose, and what the best students will think. Next, pair up with a colleague and share what you decided with each other. Have several pairs to volunteer their insights to the entire study group.

Random/plandom

Pages 83–85 of the book discuss the "structural" things teachers do or do not do to plan for success, such as grouping students together, seating charts, and proximity control. In small groups of three to five, create a list of ten additional and specific classroom occurrences which may happen as a result of a teacher who did not plan carefully for a successful lesson, situation, or behavior. Spend 10 to 15 minutes on this. In this time, you should also create a list of ten classroom occurrences that result from teachers carefully planning for successful learning and behavior. Place these brainstorming lists of two pieces of chart paper labeled "Random" and "Plandom." Have each group post its chart on a wall. One person from each group should present his or her group's lists to the whole group.

Notes

Taking It Back

Choose one concept from these two chapters that you find laudable as well as transferable to your own classroom and incorporate it into your daily professional life. Record your progress toward this goal in your Study Guide over the next few weeks, noting specific examples where you used this concept in your classroom. Arrange through your principal and a colleague you respect to observe in that colleague's room for 20 minutes one day. You should identify ways in which this colleague practices the tenets of "plandomness" over "randomness." Write these down and share them at the next session.

_____

_____

_____

_____

_____

_____

_____

_____

_____

_____

_____

_____

_____

_____

_____

_____

_____

_____

_____

_____

_____

Section Ten

Chapter 13: In Every Situation, Ask Who Is Most Comfortable and Who Is Least Comfortable

Understanding Key Concepts

- Great teachers avoid lecturing the entire class about rules and never punish the entire class because of the behavior of a few students.
- Great teachers know that the best students will feel uncomfortable if a teacher yells or uses cutting remarks, even when directed at a student who is misbehaving.
- Effective educators attempt to make people who do the right thing feel comfortable. They reinforce such people and such behaviors.
- Effective teachers never place the very best students in the position of being uncomfortable for doing the right thing.
- Great teachers treat everyone as if they are good and continually ask themselves who is most comfortable and who is least comfortable with each decision they make.

Selecting Questions for Discussion

- What is the one internal standard that supports effective practices when making decisions which follow no clearly stated rule?

- Explain the flawed thinking in sending home a note to all parents about a policy being broken by only a handful of those same parents.

- What happens when people are made to feel uncomfortable? What happens when people feel comfortable?

- Why is it unwise for teachers to have students "trade and grade" each other's schoolwork?

- How should teachers apply the "most comfortable/least comfortable" ground rule when dealing with belligerent parents?

Notes

Eliciting Journal Responses

On page 101, the book refers to a "Pay for Performance" program in use at a university and the varying reactions to the program based on a survey of all participants. The author suggests that the perspective of the entire faculty should not be the decisive factor. Instead, he advises surveying only the top one-third of the faculty to solicit their level of comfort with the program. Explain why he suggests this and how it relates to the chapter title. Think of a situation at your own school where you have felt uncomfortable with an action that you believe was taken as a response to poor performance on the part of mediocre teachers. How did this make you feel? What could have been done differently to address the problem?

_____

_____

_____

_____

_____

_____

_____

_____

_____

_____

_____

_____

_____

_____

_____

_____

_____

_____

_____

Interacting With Others

Dear parents

On pp. 98–99 of the book, the author shares a memo he saw sent home to all parents regarding picking up their children on time. He includes an alternative letter that is just as effective a reminder to the parents who are the problem while reinforcing the good behavior of the majority of the parents. In groups of three to five, brainstorm other issues that arise each year that result in a letter home to parents (e.g., attendance, signing and returning paperwork, tardies, making up work, discipline, sending children with appropriate materials). Each group should choose one topic and write two versions of a letter to parents addressing the issue. The first letter should be written using the "traditional" approach of targeting all parents equally. The second letter should be written in the alternative style, attempting to make the parents who act correctly feel comfortable, while (perhaps) making the others feel slightly uncomfortable in the hopes they will change the behavior.

Dealing with difficult parents

On p. 100, the book discusses the fact that when a belligerent parent engages a teacher in an argument, it is often the teacher, not the parent, who feels uncomfortable. Divide your study group into five groups and assign one of the following tips for dealing with difficult parents to each group:

1. Approach difficult situations and difficult parents with an attitude of respect and a willingness to listen. Remember that you and the parent have one thing in common—the desire for the parent's child to succeed.

2. Address specific complaints with ideas about what you and the parent can do together to find a solution.

3. Exercise empathy—always take some time to walk in the parent's shoes and try to gain an understanding of his or her perspective.

4. Express an attitude that is pleasant, not defensive or negative.

5. Keep tense conversations focused on the child by saying, "I care about your child." This will not only soften a difficult parent's attitude, but it will also prevent you from feeling persecuted.

Each group should examine its assigned tip and report back to the large group its thoughts on the suggestion. Brainstorm situations in which you could employ the technique and role play a situation in which you practice the suggestion. After each group has presented its "assigned" tip, as for volunteers to share other effective ways of dealing with difficult parents. Remember that great teachers do not fall into the trap of arguing with parents or responding defensively.

Notes

Taking It Back

Upon returning to your regular work setting, examine any student handbooks, parent communications, course outlines, syllabi, and codes of conduct you can locate. Examine each of the available documents and apply the *Who is most comfortable and who is least comfortable in this situation?* standard. Find any examples of language that might make your best stakeholders feel uncomfortable while doing little to address those who might truly need to understand the directives and change their behavior. Bring back any examples you can find to the next study session.

_____

_____

_____

_____

_____

_____

_____

_____

_____

_____

_____

_____

_____

_____

_____

_____

_____

_____

_____

_____

Section Eleven

Chapter 14: What About These Darn Standardized Tests?

Understanding Key Concepts

◆ Effective teachers do not allow hot-button issues to shift their focus from what really matters.

◆ Effective teachers do not allow standardized tests to take over the entire class, yet they work toward student success in the area of standardized testing so that it does not become the primary focus of the entire school.

◆ Effective teachers never allow their personal views regarding standardized testing to affect discussions they might have with their students, parents, or even peers.

◆ Effective teachers recognize that state standards force them to shift the focus from the textbook to the actual curriculum and student learning.

◆ Great teachers do not merely hold up standards and watch students make their way toward them; instead, great teachers remain at their students' sides, helping them to develop the skills they need to meet the standards.

Selecting Questions for Discussion

♦ What are two key questions we should ask in determining the role of standardized tests? What is the relationship between these two questions?

♦ In the study cited in the book, what was the difference between schools that exceeded expectations on standardized tests and schools that didn't exceed expectations?

♦ What is a risk associated with making state standards the focus of the school?

♦ What things influence what is taught in any classroom? Which of these things is the single most important determinant for what happens in the classroom and why?

♦ In the matter of standardized testing—and any other potentially controversial topic—how do the most-effective educators deal with the issue when talking with parents, students, and peers?

Notes

Eliciting Journal Responses

At the end of the chapter, the author shares a key question he posed with teachers at a school wishing to raise their reading scores: "Are you so interested in improving your students' reading abilities that you are willing to change what you do in your classroom, or do you want to raise their test scores *so that you don't have to change* what you do in your classroom?" Write about your reaction to the question he poses. By posing this question, what is the author hinting at in terms of what is important to teachers about standardized tests? Are most teachers willing to change what it is they do in their classrooms? If so, why? If not, why not? What, ultimately, should determine whether or not we change our classroom practices?

_____

_____

_____

_____

_____

_____

_____

_____

_____

_____

_____

_____

_____

_____

_____

_____

_____

_____

_____

_____

Interacting With Others

Two key questions

The book suggests that it is time to move away from debating the merits of standardized testing and to focus, instead, on our behaviors related to the issue of testing. In groups of five or fewer, discuss the two key questions the book poses: (a) What should our schools be doing? (b) What do standardized tests measure? Each group should portray its answers pictorially, using a framework similar to that offered in Figure 14-2 on p. 109 of the book. Have each group describe those things that standardized tests fail to measure but which are vitally important to any school by creating a "Top 10" list of the most important things schools must do, but which are not measured by standardized testing. At the same time, have each group create another "Top 10" list that offers the most important reasons for schools to demonstrate success on standardized tests. Have groups draw their circles and write their "Top 10" lists on chart paper. Ask each group to present their findings.

The role of standards

This chapter reminds us that standards-based education is a rapidly growing movement within the larger movement of educational reform. Briefly stated, standards-based education calls for a clear identification of what students should know and be able to do. Research shows that the amount of time spent on a specific topic can range dramatically from classroom to classroom—even at the same grade level and at the same school. The reason for this variation is, inevitably, teacher preference. With this in mind, divide into small groups that are clustered as closely as possible based on similar subject areas and/or grade levels. You will be looking at examples of clearly written performance standards currently in place at different schools. Once in groups, pick one subject and grade level with which all participants are comfortable. Examine the distributed standards and within each group, create a simplified list of five standards that are absolutely essential areas of learning for students at that grade level. Share these five standards with the large group as a starting point for discussing the value of clearly identified critical knowledge and skills that must be learned in varying subjects at each grade level.

Notes

Taking It Back

Using Figures 14-1 and 14-2 on pp. 108–109 of the book as a guiding reference, ask five teachers and/or administrators whom you respect to answer the two questions the author poses. In addition, specifically ask these five educators: What things are we doing at our school that are not measured by standardized tests but still vitally important? Are there things that the standardized tests measure that we as a school are not doing? What percentage of what we do at school is measured by standardized tests? What *should* that percentage be? What behaviors must we agree on in order to ensure success on standardized tests? Be prepared to share the feedback you receive at the next session.

Section Twelve

Chapter 15:
Make It Cool to Care
Chapter 16: Clarifying Your Core

Understanding Key Concepts

- All effective teachers have a core set of beliefs to which they adhere as educators.
- Getting faculty members to go along with the latest trend or mandate has limited value; instead, the key is to develop and establish a schoolwide environment that supports everyone's efforts to do what is right.
- The real challenge—and the real accomplishment—is to get all the students to care about what happens in the classroom, and to create an atmosphere in which it is "cool to care."
- In great schools, the teachers tell stories about what other teachers have accomplished with students.
- Great teachers do what is right, no matter what else is going on.
- Great educators understand that behaviors and beliefs are tied to emotion, and they understand the power of emotion to jump-start change.
- Students care about great teachers because they know that great teachers care about them.
- Without a core of firmly held beliefs, it is difficult for teachers to steer a steady course.
- With this core, teachers feel secure and confident. More importantly, so do their students.
- Every teacher has an impact. Great teachers make a difference.

Selecting Questions for Discussion

- Why is it so important to establish a classroom environment in which it is "cool to care"?

- What is one thing that great teachers can choose to do when colleagues make sarcastic, derogatory comments?

- What must we as teachers do with students before we can connect with their minds?

- As a principal, why did the author decide to cease the practice of collecting lesson plans from teachers? Can you think of current or past practices that may be similar?

- Describe the framework that sustains the work of all great educators.

- Of the "Fourteen Things That Matter Most" listed as a summary on p. 127 of the book, which do you feel is the foremost essential practice? Why?

Eliciting Journal Responses

On p. 116 of the book, the author describes "The Great Teacher" he identifies as "Mrs. Heart." How did Mrs. Heart motivate Darin to become interested in poetry? What were Mrs. Heart's attitudes toward the state standards, standardized tests, and new initiatives that were inevitably rolled out over the years? In your own words, what was Mrs. Heart's philosophy of education? Is this a philosophy with which you agree? Take a moment to describe your own philosophy of education after reading this book.

_____

_____

_____

_____

_____

_____

_____

_____

_____

_____

_____

_____

_____

_____

_____

_____

_____

_____

_____

_____

_____

_____

Interacting With Others

14 Things

Have each of the "Fourteen Things That Matter Most" on a separate slip of paper. Tape each of the items on a separate desk around the room. Divide into 14 groups (or have them work individually if there are 14 or fewer participants). Each group will start at one of the 14 "stations" and spend 5 minutes reflecting on the item at that desk. Write down examples from the book or your own experience that relate to the statement. Write down why you feel the statement is important. After five minutes, the group will rotate one desk (moving in numerical order, with those people at desk #14 rotating to desk #1). Repeat the process of reflecting on each statement until each participant/group has moved through all 14 stations.

Clarifying your core

After reviewing the author's core beliefs, think about additional core beliefs not mentioned in the book that you personally believe are essential components of your personal mission as a teacher. Write down between two and four additional core beliefs you value as an educator. Pair up with another participant and share each other's core belief additions. Ask for volunteers to share their beliefs with the whole group.

Notes

Taking It Back

On p. 119 of the book, it states that in great schools teachers tell stories about the teaching legends with whom they have worked. Write about one or more teachers at your current school you consider a "legendary" teacher. Also write about a teacher in your own life who positively impacted you and who you also consider a legend. Share these written stories with the teacher you are writing about by placing it in that teacher's mailbox. In the case of your own teacher who you looked up to, mail the writing to that former teacher or to one of that person's family members.

_____

_____

_____

_____

_____

_____

_____

_____

_____

_____

_____

_____

_____

_____

_____

_____

_____

_____

_____

_____

_____

_____

Fourteen Things That Matter Most

1. Great teachers never forget that it is people, not programs, that determine the quality of a school.
2. Great teachers establish clear expectations at the start of the year and follow them consistently as the year progresses.
3. When a student misbehaves, great teachers have one goal: to keep that behavior from happening again.
4. Great teachers have high expectations for students but even higher expectations for themselves.
5. Great teachers know who is the variable in the classroom: *They are.* Good teachers consistently strive to improve, and they focus on something they can control—their own performance.
6. Great teachers create a positive atmosphere in their classrooms and schools. They treat every person with respect. In particular, they understand the power of praise.
7. Great teachers consistently filter out the negatives that don't matter and share a positive attitude.
8. Great teachers work hard to keep their relationships in good repair—to avoid personal hurt and to repair any possible damage.
9. Great teachers have the ability to ignore trivial disturbances and the ability to respond to inappropriate behavior without escalating the situation.
10. Great teachers have a plan and purpose for everything they do. If things don't work out they way they had envisioned, they reflect on what they could have done differently and adjust their plans accordingly.
11. Before making any decision or attempting to bring about any change, great teachers ask themselves one central question: *What will the best people think?*
12. Great teachers continually ask themselves who is most comfortable and who is least comfortable with each decision they make. They treat everyone as if they were good.
13. Great teachers keep standardized testing in perspective; they center on the real issue of student learning.
14. Great teachers care about their students. They understand that behaviors and beliefs are tied to emotion, and they understand the power of emotion to jump-start change.

If you would like information about inviting Todd Whitaker to speak to your group, please contact him at t-whitaker@indstate.edu or at his web site www.toddwhitaker.com or (812) 237-2904.

If you enjoyed this book, we recommend:

Seven Simple Secrets:
What the BEST Teachers Know and Do
Annette Breaux & Todd Whitaker

"Easy to read and with great use of humor, this is a wonderful book for new teachers and their mentors."

Sharon Weber, Principal
Bell Township Elementary School, PA

Implementing these secrets will change your life both in and out of the classroom. But most importantly, they will enhance the lives of every student you teach!

This book reveals—

- The Secret of Planning

- The Secret of Classroom Management

- Secret of Instruction

- The Secret of Attitude

- The Secret of Professionalism

- The Secret of Effective Discipline

- The Secret of Motivation and Inspiration

2006. 150 pp. (est.) Paperback. 1-59667-021-5. $29.95 plus shipping and handling.

Order form on page 89

Great Quotes for Great Educators
Todd Whitaker and Dale Lumpa

Over 600 insightful, witty nuggets to motivate and inspire you…

…and everyone else at your school.

Teachers—display these quotes in your classrooms!

Administrators—insert them into your faculty memos and share them at staff meetings!

Why is this book *unique?*

♦ includes over 100 original quotes from internationally acclaimed speaker and educator Todd Whitaker

♦ features real quotes from real students, which echo wit and wisdom for educators

♦ each quote has a direct connection to your life as an educator

Examples of quotes in this book…

"Great teachers have high expectations for their students, but higher expectations for themselves."

Todd Whitaker

"We can never control a classroom until we control ourselves."

Todd Whitaker

2004, 150 pp. (est) paperback 1-903556-82-9 $29.95 plus shipping and handling

Order form on page 89

Teaching Matters:
Motivating & Inspiring Yourself
Todd and Beth Whitaker

"This book makes you want to be the best teacher you can be."

Nancy Fahnstock,
Godby High School
Tallahassee, Florida

Celebrate the teaching life! This book helps teachers:

♦ rekindle the excitement of the first day of school all year long

♦ approach every day in a "Thank God it is Monday" frame of mind

♦ not let negative people ruin your day

♦ fall in love with teaching all over again

Brief Contents

♦ Why You're Worth it

♦ Unexpected Happiness

♦ Could I Have a Refill Please? (Opportunities for Renewal)

♦ Celebrating Yourself

♦ Raise the Praise–Minimize the Criticize

♦ Making School Work for You

2002, 150 pp. paperback 1-930556-35-7 $24.95 plus shipping and handling

Order form on page 89

What Great Principals Do Differently:
15 Things That Matter Most

Todd Whitaker

"... affirming and uplifting, with insights into human nature and 'real people' examples..."

Edward Harris, Principal
Chetek High School, WI

What are the specific qualities and practices of great principals that elevate them above the rest? Blending school-centered studies and experience working with hundreds of administrators, Todd Whitaker reveals why these practices are effective and demonstrates how to implement each of them in your school.

Brief Contents

- It's People, Not Programs
- Who is the Variable?
- Hire Great Teachers
- Standardized Testing
- Focus on Behavior, Then Focus on Beliefs
- Base Every Decision on Your Best Teachers
- Make it Cool to Care
- Set Expectations At the Start of the Year
- Clarifying Your Core

2002, 130 pp. paperback 1-930556-47-0 $29.95 plus shipping and handling

Order form on page 89

Dealing with Difficult Teachers
Second Edition
Todd Whitaker

"…filled with inspirational ideas and strategies that work."

Melanie Brock, Principal
Westview Elementary School
Excelsior Springs, MO

Whether you are a teacher, administrator, or fill some other role in your school, difficult teachers can make your life miserable. This book shows you how to handle staff members who:

♦ gossip in the teacher's lounge.

♦ consistently say "it won't work" when any new idea is suggested.

♦ undermine your efforts toward school improvement.

♦ negatively influence other staff members.

Added to this edition are 4 new chapters on communicating with difficult teachers.

This new section demonstrates how to:

♦ eliminate negative behaviors.

♦ implement effective questioning strategies.

♦ apply the "The Best Teacher/Worst Teacher" test.

2002, 208 pp. paperback 1-930556-45-4 $29.95 plus shipping and handling

Order form on page 89

Motivating and Inspiring Teachers:
The Educational Leader's Guide for Building Staff Morale

Todd Whitaker, Beth Whitaker, and Dale Lumpa

"The most appealing feature of this book is its simplicity and common sense. It is practical, useful and readable, and I recommend it."

Ron Seckler, Principal
Swope Middle School, NV

Filled with strategies to motivate and stimulate your staff, this book features simple suggestions that you can integrate into your current daily routines. It will show you how to:

- insert key phrases and specific actions into your day-to-day conversations, staff meetings, and written memos to stimulate peak effectiveness

- hire new staff and plan orientation and induction meetings to cultivate and retain loyal and motivated staff members

- use the "gift of time" to stimulate and reward

- get amazing results by not taking credit for them

- motivate yourself each and every day

2000, 252 pp. paperback 1-883001-99-4 $34.95 plus shipping and handling

Order form on page 89

Feeling Great!
The Educator's Guide for Eating Better, Exercising Smarter, and Feeling Your Best

Todd Whitaker and Jason Winkle

"This book will *especially* appeal to people who do not like to exercise."

Katherine Alvestad
Dowell Elementary School, MD

Educator's spend so much time taking care of others that we sometimes forget to take care of ourselves! This book will help teachers, principals, professors, and all educators find time in our busy schedules to focus on our physical self. You will learn how to:

♦ make time for exercise in your hectic daily schedule.

♦ learn how to feel your best every day.

♦ eat right even when on the go.

♦ keep your fitness momentum going all yea.

♦ turn your daily routines into healthy habits.

Brief Contents

♦ Why Fitness for Educators? What's So Special About Us?

♦ But I Don't Like to Sweat

♦ Setting Realistic Goals

♦ Finding the Time and the Energy

♦ Keeping it up Through the Summer

♦ Fad or Fact? What Diets Really Work?

2002, 150 pp. paperback 1-930556-38-1 $24.95 plus shipping and handling

Order form on page 89

Dealing with Difficult Parents
(And with Parents in Difficult Situations)
Todd Whitaker & Douglas J. Fiore

"This book is an easy read with common sense appeal. The authors are not afraid to share their own vulnerability and often demonstrate a sense of humor."

Gale Hulme, Program Director
Georgia's Leadership Institute
for School Improvement

This book helps teachers, principals, and other educators develop skills in working with the most difficult parents in the most challenging situations. It shows you how to:

- avoid the "trigger" words that serve only to make bad situations worse.

- use the right words and phrases to help you develop more positive relationships with parents.

- deal with parents who accuse you of not being fair.

- build positive relationships with even the most challenging parents.

2001, 175 pp. paperback 1-930556-09-8 $29.95 plus shipping and handling

Order form on page 89

Six Types of Teachers
Recruiting, Retaining and Mentoring the Best
Douglas J. Fiore and Todd Whitaker

"The examples of the six types of teachers are awesome! This book is a valuable resource for all those engaged in hiring and retaining teachers."

Jeff Remelius,
Rogers Middle School, MO

This book sharpens your ability to hire new teachers, improve the ones already there, and keep your best and brightest on board.

Among the types of teachers revealed are the **WOWs** (the ones who walk on water); the **Solids** (dependable, hardworking contributors to the good of the school); the ones who are "not bad" but **Replaceable** ... and more.

2005, 176 pp. paperback. 1-930556-85-3. $29.95 plus shipping and handling.

Order form on page 89

Interested in ordering multiple copies of Eye On Education titles?

- ◆ Order copies as "welcome" gifts for all of your *new* teachers
- ◆ Order copies as holiday gifts for *all* of your teachers
- ◆ Assign them as required reading in new teacher induction programs
- ◆ Assign them in book study groups with experienced teachers

Our discount schedule —

			Discount
10–24	copies	=	5%
25–74	copies	=	10%
75–99	copies	=	15%
100–199	copies	=	20%
200–299	copies	=	25%
300–399	copies	=	30%

More? Call us or visit our website.

(plus shipping and handling.)

Note: These discounts apply to orders of individual titles and do not apply to combinations of more than one title.

6 Depot Way West
Larchmont, NY 10538
Phone (888) 299-5350
Fax (914) 833-0761
www.eyeoneducation.com

ORDER FORM

GUARANTEE! If you are not satisfied with any book, simply return it within 30 days in saleable condition for full credit or refund.

☐SEVEN SIMPLE SECRETS: What the BEST Teachers Know and Do. Breaux and Whitaker. 2006. 150 pp. paper. 1-59667-021-5. $29.95 plus shipping and handling.

☐WHAT GREAT TEACHERS DO DIFFERENTLY: 14 Things That Matter Most. Whitaker. 2004. 144 pp. paper. 1-930556-69-1. $29.95 plus shipping and handling.

☐STUDY GUIDE: WHAT GREAT TEACHERS DO DIFFERENTLY. Whitaker and Whitaker. 2006. 86 pp. paper. 1-59667-024-X. $16.95 plus shipping and handling.

☐DEALING WITH DIFFICULT PARENTS (AND WITH PARENTS IN DIFFICULT SITUATIONS). Whitaker and Fiore. 2001. 175 pp. paper. 1-930556-09-8. $29.95 plus shipping and handling.

☐TEACHING MATTERS: Motivating and Inspiring Yourself. Whitaker and Whitaker. 2002. 150 pp. paper. 1-930556-35-7. $24.95 plus s and h.

☐MOTIVATING AND INSPIRING TEACHERS: The Educational Leader's Guide for Building Staff Morale. Whitaker, Whitaker, and Lumpa. 2000. 252 pp. paper. 1-883001-99-4. $34.95 plus shipping and handling.

☐FEELING GREAT! The Educator's Guide for Eating Better, Exercising Smarter, and Feeling Your Best. Whitaker and Winkle. 2002. 150 pp. paper. 1-930556-38-1. $24.95 plus shipping and handling.

☐WHAT GREAT PRINCIPALS DO DIFFERENTLY: 15 Things That Matter Most. Whitaker. 2002. 130 pp. paper. 1-930556-47-0. $29.95 plus shipping and handling.

☐DEALING WITH DIFFICULT TEACHERS, Second Edition. Whitaker. 2002. 208 pp. paper. 1-930556-45-4. $29.95 plus s and h.

☐SIX TYPES OF TEACHERS: Recruiting, Retaining, and Mentoring the Best. Fiore and Whitaker. 2005. 176 pp. paper. 1-930556-85-3. $29.95 plus shipping and handling.

☐GREAT QUOTES FOR GREAT EDUCATORS. Whitaker and Lumpa. 2004. 208 pp. paper. 1-930556-82-9. $29.95 plus shipping and handling.

☐Save $30! Order all 11 books for $281.45 plus shipping and handling.

METHOD OF PAYMENT (choose one):   ☐Check (enclosed)   ☐Credit Card   ☐Purchase Order

Shipping and Handling
1 book - Add $6.00
2 books - Add $10.00
3 books - Add $13.00
4 books - Add $15.00
5–7 books - Add $17.00
8–11 books - Add $19.00
12–15 books - Add $25.00
More: Feel free to call or visit our web site.

N.Y. and N.J. residents add sales tax. Prices subject to change without notice.

6 Depot Way West
Larchmont, NY 10538
PHONE (888) 299-5350
FAX (914) 833-0761
www.eyeoneducation.com

| Purchase Order # or Credit Card # with exp. Date (Visa, MasterCard, or Discover) | Your e-mail address (for free excerpts form new and future titles) |

SHIPPING ADDRESS   SCHOOL?   HOME?   **BILLING ADDRESS FOR PURCHASE ORDERS**

Name _____   Name _____

School _____   School _____

Street Address _____   Street Address _____

City _____ State ____ Zip ____   City _____ State ____ Zip ____

Phone _____   Phone _____

Your Job Title: ☐ Principal   ☐ Teacher   ☐ District   ☐ Administrator   ☐ Other   SG